TESTIMONIAL

"I had the privilege of studying with Felice, and I can't speak highly enough about his guidance. He is incredibly patient and truly in connection with spirit, which makes every session feel grounded and insightful. His straightforward approach helps me navigate complex topics with clarity, and no question is ever too small or unimportant for him to answer. Felice is not just a teacher; he is a phenomenal mentor who is always there, offering unwavering support on my spiritual journey. I am deeply grateful for his wisdom and the profound impact he has had on my life." **Tanya Sage**

DISCOVERING YOURSELF

THROUGH MEDIUMSHIP
DEVELOPMENT CLASSES

Learning to be Happy, Healthy, Whole and Alive

REV. FELICE IZZARELLI

Cover & Layout by Michael Grossman

Publisher's Information

For information On Development classes, call: 760 580 9459

www.experiential-evolution.com

Author contact: FeliceIzzarelli@gmail.com

ISBN 978-1-953080-62-2

Experiential Evolution

TABLE OF CONTENTS

PREFACE

Mediumship Development

In this book, we will be exploring the Laws of the Universe and examining some of the different aspects of Mental Mediumship which includes: Clairvoyance, Clairaudience, Clairsentience, Psychometry, and learning about your Guides, Teachers, and the roles they play in your life.

This will be a hands-on class and we will also look at different aspects of **Physical Mediumship**. For instance: What is ectoplasm? Where does it come from? How does it work with your body and why do you need it for table tipping?

We will discuss how important meditation is to your spiritual growth; for without meditation, you will only go so far. You will discover much about yourself and your higher consciousness and reconnect to the magic within.

What is Spirit Mediumship?

A medium is one who is sensitive to the vibrations of the spirit world and able to convey messages and produce the phenomena of spirit.

Are mediums born at birth or can they be developed?

Experience has taught us to believe that our best mediums were such from birth, and what we have heard from their childhood experience leads us to believe that is the case. Sometimes, however, someone may have a dramatic incident that occurs in their life, such as a near death experience or a healing, that opens oneself to the spirit world. Spirit teacher tells us that each individual has this mediumship ability which can be developed by meditation, studying the world of spirit, and by getting to know oneself, that God self within. We don't always get the phase of Mediumship that we think we should have, but we do receive the one that is always for our best and highest good.

A Few of the Different Types of Mental Mediumship

1. **Clairvoyance:** a French word for "clear seeing" with the spirit eye or the third eye (one and the same). You can see spirit symbols and sometimes names written in the ethers (etheric realm). Some teachers place clairvoyance, clairaudience, and clairsentience under one general heading of clairvoyance.

2. **CLAIRAUDIENCE:** "clear hearing" - the ability to hear with your spirit ear or 'inner' ear. One is able to hear spirit teachers and loved ones that have crossed over.

3. **CLAIRSENTIENCE:** soul sense – the ability to sense spirit people around and to receive their impressions. Clairsentience may be one of the least discussed yet most important phases of the work you must learn to distinguish clairsentience from imagination.

4. **PSYCHOMETRY:** the ability to hold an object and pick up its vibration, to give names and messages from loved ones who have crossed over, and to understand symbols connected to the spirit realm.

Something to Keep in Mind as You Develop Spiritually

It is important to be aware of the need for continued education so one may advance physically, mentally, and spiritually. If one does not continue their education, they may become quite frustrated or puzzled because they have not progressed beyond the initial development of the first year or two. They often end up withdrawing from study or further investigation and begin to feel secure and happy in their own types of Mediumship, such as automatic writing, message giving, or advice. When they attend séances, they often make a big show of their own powers, though usually this reflects their own thought patterns or ego.

Here are some words of advice for anyone who sits in a class for spiritual development or enlightenment. I have found people who step onto this path go through four stages. There are a few rare exceptions, but it is wise that you become aware of and understand the different stages one might go through.

FOUR STAGES

FIRST STAGE: the person becomes an investigator and searches for 'proof' that the spiritual realm is real, in order to remove doubt and skepticism. This is a stage of great questioning where one can become either easily diverted or a sincere seeker of truth.

SECOND STAGE: the person becomes very eager to learn. This period usually lasts approximately 6 to 12 months. During this time, the newcomer is filled with excitement and enthusiasm and endeavors to share his new found knowledge with everyone. Here the person is positive that every sign and every little breeze or sound are the result of spirit manifestations. These people sometimes force messages upon friends, family and co-workers which may or may not be welcomed. They can disturb their friends' happy lives by relaying all kinds of unwanted messages.

THIRD STAGE: having successfully survived the second stage, they start to realize that there is something more to Mediumship than just talking with spirit and giving messages. They start to attend classes, and sit in meditation, prayer. They begin studying every free moment they have. Many think they have lost time in their development. This is a misconception because everything happens in Divine timing, nothing is ever lost.

FOURTH STAGE: This is the stage which all should seek to achieve: coming in touch with the higher self while on the Earth. It is the true endeavor of spirit work. The few who do, see this and realize it, want to attain it. This sets them apart from the others. When you reach this level, you learn the meaning of the statement: in this world, but not of it. They do not speak of their development in psychic terms. They are satisfied to know that their spiritual progression, and absolute control of self has taken place in their life. They apply this training to their Earthly life. They are humble and understanding of others and of themselves.

Words of criticism, slander, and gossip find no place in their soul or their lives. They give freely of their strength and knowledge and seek no return from the ones they help. They have learned and received this simple truth, that in the knowing of knowing, God is the infinite intelligence and nothing is impossible for God to do.

PRAYER

As you start doing your Mediumship work, it is important to always open up with a prayer and ask for the best and highest good. Whether you are working with someone, doing a circle, or simply sitting at home with friends, prayer is very important. It helps you set your intentions. Don't worry how it sounds, or if you feel like the words are not just right, spirit knows when it comes from the heart and that's what is important. After you're done working with your teachers and guides, remember to do a closing prayer and give thanks for the wonderful energies and the light that was present in the room with you. Think of it like this, when you call up and invite a family member or good friend into your home, you welcome them. When the evening is done you say your goodbyes and you wish them well and more than likely, you thank them for coming over. This brings closure to the evening. The same is true with spirit.

When you start with an opening prayer and a closing prayer, go into silence for a moment and hear the words that speak from your heart…for you really do know them.

Here is a prayer that I feel can be used both for the opening and closing.

God bless all those who sent their blessings fourth. Thank you, God for all the trials and troubles, for it is by these that we grow and progress. Thank you, God for the good that comes to us and may we ever remember to share with others along the way. May the light of the Divine brighten your path, now and for always. Amen

A closing prayer: We give thanks for the time that we have spent with you, Spirit, for the love you have shared with us today. We ask that you continue to bring the light of peace and joy throughout the week to all of us and for all that come into our lives. Amen

Another option is one of my favorites for the opening and closing prayer:

The Lord's Prayer

> *Our Father in heaven, hallowed be your name, your kingdom come, your will be done, on earth as it is in heaven. Give us this day our daily bread. And forgive us for our trespasses, as we forgive those who trespass against us. And lead us not into temptation, but deliver us from evil For thine is the kingdom and the power and the glory forever and ever."*

MEDITATIONS

It is wise to set a specific time of day for your meditation, whether you're a beginner or you have been doing this for a while. You will be making a commitment to time set aside for yourself and your teachers. At times our life may be very busy, so remember that meditation doesn't need to be long to provide results: 5 to 15 minutes is enough. That is not really much time out of 24 hours. You'll find that when you do this on a consistent basis, it will bring peace and joy into your life, and the worries of the day won't seem so bad.

Meditation helps you to connect with your teachers, guides, and your higher self. This is one of the ways to develop your Mediumship skills. Take a look at it this way: when you call to set up an appointment with your doctor, dentist, or even maybe to get a massage, you know that person will be there at that time. It is the same way with spirit, that one-on-one time that you have set aside is like an appointment. Yes, we do have spirit around us, but it's a big Universe out there, and at times they do have other things to do. Meditation has additional benefits that I am sure you will find out as you practice.

When you meditate you can put music on or not, the choice is yours; it's what you feel comfortable with. Find a place to meditate in a chair or even laying down but remember not to fall asleep. Find a sacred spot in your home for your meditations. Make sure that you will not be disturbed – turn off your phone.

What follows is a meditation that I like to do which helps me to connect to my teachers or new guides that have come in to help me. If you have trouble remembering this meditation, find yourself a recorder or create a voice memo on your phone and tape it in your own words.

TEMPLE MEDITATIONS

Find a comfortable position and start by taking a few deep, slow breaths. As you inhale, visualize white light entering your body; as you exhale, allow the stress of the day to flow out of you. As you inhale again, visualize a white light filling your very being, your very soul; and as you exhale, relax and release. Inhale again and feel the white light warming you from within. You're feeling nice and relaxed, as if an electric blanket is wrapped around you. The warmth, the peacefulness, and the calmness embrace you. You feel at one with yourself. Look into your mind's eye, your third eye, located in the center of your forehead, and as you do this, you see the Universe unfolding to you. You feel peaceful and relaxed.

Within your mind's eye, see yourself arising out of your body, up through the ceiling, up through the roof. Look around and see the familiar sights around you, as you keep rising up through the sky into the Universe. As you gaze in front of you, you see a beautiful temple. The temple is white and it has a gold dome on top. There are white stairs leading to the door. Look at the door. It is beautiful. Solid oak, with a beautiful finish. The door feels so smooth. Knock on this great door. It slowly opens. Within, you see that a new teacher stands before you. You call your teacher by name or the teacher may give you their name. As you walk into the temple, look around, seeing many hallways and many rooms.

The teacher tells you that each room has a special purpose, and you are free to choose to enter any of the rooms you wish. You may choose to go into the room that is for healing, or maybe you prefer the lecture room where many are gathered. There is also a beautiful, lush garden where you can talk to your teacher or teachers and receive the answers that you have come for. This can be for 5 or 15 minutes or for long as you like. This is your time.

When you are finished, walk back to the front of the temple. Thank your teacher for their time and for the answers that have been given to you. Walking back outside, you feel a sense of satisfaction and completion. Turn one last time to say thank you to your teacher and you watch as the door slowly closes. You know that you can come back to this beautiful temple at any time. As you leave the temple and walk back down the steps, you start to become aware again of the Universe, and you know it is time to return home. Slowly, you drift back into the blue skies of the Earth. You see the trees and buildings that are familiar. You float back down through the roof, through the ceiling, and back into your body. Slowly, become more aware of your surroundings. As you begin to awake, you remember everything that was said and given to you. You feel refreshed, awakened and at peace with yourself, for you know this journey has been completed.

A Collective God Bush

The true self develops like a beautiful rose:
from a seed to the roots, to the spreading of each limb and each leaf, until the bud unfolds
and each pedal reveals the Wholeness of the God-Self.

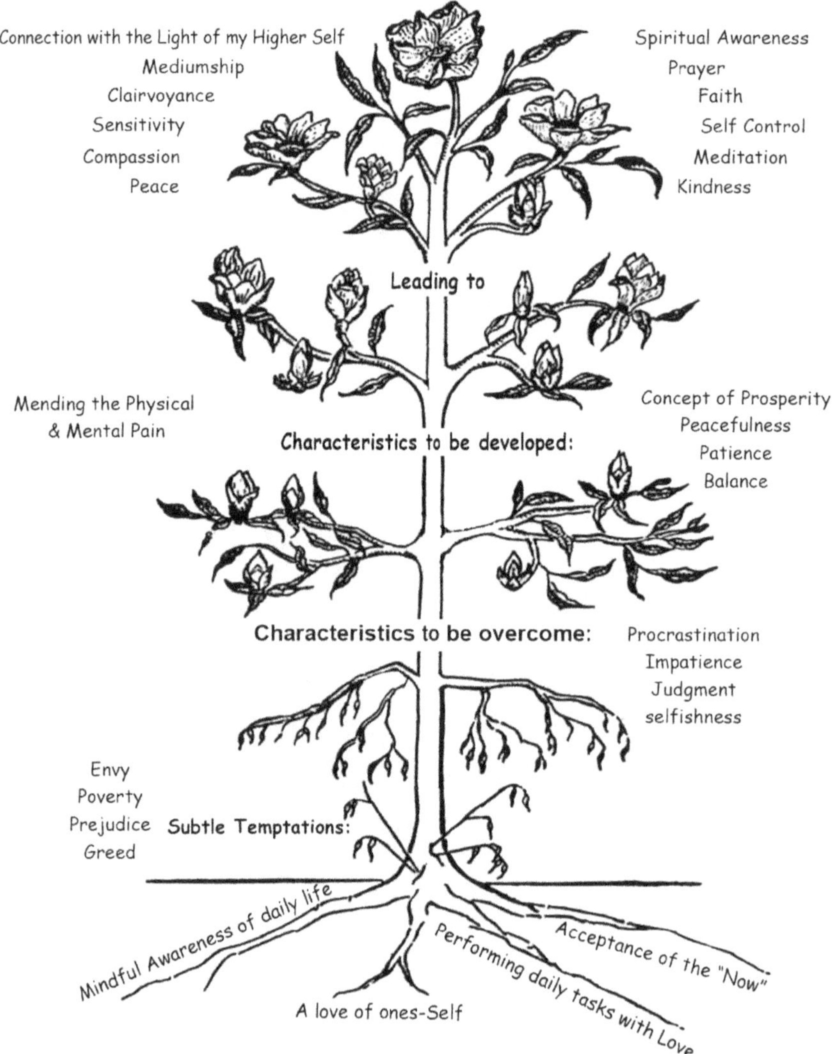

MESSAGE FROM SPIRIT

You have been surrounded with everything you need to make you happy. It is up to you to reach for the sky or look into the corners of the Earth, in search of your happiness. Search within your higher consciousness and within your own surroundings for your higher development and conditions that will elevate and permit you to unfold your higher self, that God-given spark of beauty within.

Listen to how your higher consciousness is calling to you with the message of beauty and inspiration. It's like the coming of spring, the unfolding of leaves, the springing forth of grass and all of nature's bounty that is promised. The promise is fulfilled throughout the year as it progresses. With each new season there is the promise of unfoldment, a fresh newness. There is a law that governs all souls. Make yourself receptive to the law of love, peace, and harmony in all that you do.

You will find the beauty and justice in the world and will be able to see your love and the love of God shining through you in every way. If you fail to find the light and beauty within, that God spark within, how can you hope to have a full appreciation of God's love for you?

Let's take a little journey to a beautiful place. First, we must go within to ourselves. Passing through the beautifully landscaped grounds where the grass is green and the sun shines bright, flower beds are well-placed, in keeping with the harmony and beauty of the place we are approaching. All these expressions of beauty serve to elevate our being to a state of consciousness that makes us ready to enter that wonderful place of oneness with ourselves, the higher consciousness. A place of love, peace, and harmony.

God's beauty, your inner self, is ever present and always reminding us that we have only to seek and we shall find. How can we hope for an understanding of the power of one's higher self and God's love when we bypass the beautiful things all around us? Learn to approach God through yourself on the path that has been laid out before you.

If you are unable to see love within yourself and for yourself, how can you expect the consciousness you take with you to do any more for you than that which you are doing for yourself now? You cannot expect to enter the realm of spirit with a brighter vision than you have developed here. This is the training ground, the opportunity to live. To express and progress in the physical form to a point where you will have risen with your consciousness and are ready for the realm where there is still more light and love.

Let's Get Started

As you seek you shall find. You will find a spiritual food to nourish your higher spiritual development. Each of you is a child of God. Each thought, each wish, each time you seek spiritual enlightenment, you are drawing closer to your guides and teachers and spirit.

Each of you has your own soul's purpose. The experiences your higher self has picked out for you are necessary for your spiritual progression. There are many tools placed at your disposal, to be used by you, as a means of obtaining the expression of material accomplishments. One day you will return home to God, not as a conquering hero, but as a person of great spiritual experiences. You will return to spirit carrying with you the experience and the memory of your thoughts and deeds while on the Earth plane. Yes, we can enjoy spiritual happiness and material success while on the Earth plane.

As you reach out for the higher vibrations and look into yourself, you open the way for spirit and loved ones to come to your aid. They will assist you as you move towards the destiny which is specially designed for you. You are all passing through one of the most important phases in existence, your life; it is a great period of unfoldment. Think back on all of the interesting things you have done, the abilities that you have developed in the physical and in spiritual realms. The spirit of your soul knows that each trial you conquer brings you closer to your soul's purpose. Know that as you continue to grow in your spiritual unfoldment and understanding, you will see the purpose for all things whether they be lessons of failure, pain, or pleasure. You'll find that nothing experienced has been in vain and nothing achieved has been too small.

You have the tools for every experience in order to learn your lesson. Remember that you're preparing your home (spiritual home?) according to the way you live here. We have come to this Earth plane for our soul's journey, our higher self; we have given ourselves the opportunity to learn and to progress. Longing for something better is not enough. One must make an effort - slow, steady living better each day. (Can you please be specific about what living 'better' would look like?) When you accomplish the lesson in your own spiritual growth and know the lesson has value as you apply it - as you make use of the knowledge – only then can you say it belongs to you.

Learn who you are, a child of God, a spiritual being. These are some of the privileges given to you that you may pass to the higher connections of the higher self. If you can listen well to the voice of God within you, you will realize there is no further need to return to the Earth unless you wish to do so.

THE ROLES OF TEACHERS AND GUIDES

INNER BAND

The teachers and guides who have been with us for this incarnation and who will remain with us until we decide to cross over. Usually, five to seven guides.

Master Teachers

Master teachers are usually illumined beings. They were Masters on the Earth plane and continue to work from the spiritual realm. Each person has one; their role is to oversee our growth and spiritual development. To help us to stay on our path. All the other guides report to or work under the supervision of the master.

Protector [Your Big Indian]

These guides are usually Indians, but not always. They seem bigger than life, strong in their manner and appearance. Their role is to provide protection in our daily life and our spiritual work. They give us extra strength and energy when required.

Doctor of Philosophy [Teacher]

This spirit guide works to assist us in our spiritual growth by helping us to understand philosophy and is involved in all the studies we undertake in this life.

Chemist Doctor [Teacher]

The chemist doctor is the one that works with the chemistry of the body for Mediumship and healing. They help us by altering the chemistry of the body so that we may more easily attune to spirit vibration, and with the chemicals in the body to produce ectoplasm energy for physical Mediumship.

Healing [Teacher]

Your healing teacher is the one that helps you when you are working with others and yourself. When there is a need in your life or someone else's they bring in the healing energy to create balance physically, mentally, and spiritually.

Joy Guide

The joy guide brings laughter and joy into our lives. Sometimes when things are lost - like keys, glasses, or jewelry, and then all of a sudden you find them, it is the joy guide having a little fun. Remember when this happens to ask your joy guide to bring it back to you. It will usually put a smile on your face. Your joy guide can also be the one that brings you messages to pass on to others from their teachers. They sometimes take the form of children or youths.

Doorkeeper, Gatekeeper

This role may be filled by your protector; it's usually someone from your inner band. They help to keep the negative entities away while you work in the spirit realm. They guard the door to allow only appropriate entities for the situation to enter. They guard the physical body while the consciousness is withdrawn, for those who want to develop, deep trance, or offer the physical side of Mediumship.

Message Bearers

These guides are usually in your inner band and they help bring you the message from spirit so you can pass it on to the one who is receiving the message. Sometime other spirits will bring the message depending on the individual's needs.

OUTER BAND

The outer band is usually made up of different spirits. These spirits come in to help you when you have a specific need. To help you fix things, like the computer, you would call a computer specialist from spirit. Or if you were working on your car, you would call someone to help you with that. They help to bring specialized knowledge in. Spirit is always willing to help us, but you need to remember to ask for help.

Universal Teachers

These are Master teachers that work with many people at one time. You may have a couple master teachers that you work with, but remember that they work with many, not just one person. They work on global world issues. These master teachers have a very high vibration. Here are some examples of master teachers: St. Francis, St. Germain, Archangel Michael, White Eagle.

God gave us choice of free will, and spirit is not allowed to interfere unless we ask for help. It is important to remember to "always ask" spirit to be in your daily life to help you and to work with you. They are waiting and willing to assist us anytime we want or need them.

NOTES:

____

____

____

____

____

As you receive the names of your teachers and guides that you are working with, write them down on this page.

Your Inner Band

Master Teacher: _______________________________

Doctor of Philosophy: _______________________________

Chemist Doctor: _______________________________

Your Healer: _______________________________

Big Indian: _______________________________

Joy Guide: _______________________________

NOTES:

____

____

____

____

Outer Band

You can have many different spirits in your outer band. They come in to help with all sorts of things. The sky is the limit, but remember to keep it simple, otherwise it can get a little confusing with too much information coming in.

1.___________________________________

2.___________________________________

3.___________________________________

4.___________________________________

5.___________________________________

NOTES:

Universal Teachers

1.____

2.____

3.____

4.____

5.____

6.____

7.____

NOTES:

____

____

____

____

____

Responsibility

Have you ever asked yourself these two questions: After so many years of sitting and studying, why do I still not understand? Shouldn't I be farther along? Maybe something happened in your life that you feel wasn't for your best and highest good. It could be something as simple as you twisted your ankle, and you ask yourself, "Where were my spirit teachers and my spirit protectors?"

You need to learn that individuals are responsible for themselves. There really is no progress without acceptance of personal responsibility. This is why we sometimes have the same lessons over and over again, but within different experiences. We keep getting them until we learn them. But think how much greater the fall or intense the experience would have been if spirit was not around you.

Remember, you are in human form. You came down here for these experiences, which lead to development. Make no mistake, you will succeed in the school of life according to lessons you learn. Sometimes as you go through your studies of life, the lessons can cause distress, worry, and pain. At times you probably say to yourself, "I really could do without some of those experiences." This is when we need to look within, and to look all around one's self. When one focuses this way and really shifts into their higher self, into the silence and looks, they will be surprised at the answer they receive.

Have you ever stopped to think about children going through the lower grades? There is a process which prepares them for the understanding of a higher level of learning, as they progress through the grades which helps them grow and mature. These studies have laid the ground work. These studies have made them ready to receive and understand more advanced ideas.

Think of the great masters of this world, they were once children who had to learn the fundamentals. It is as important for you to go through this process as it is for the children. Many of the experiences which you are passing through are stepping stones preparing you for further development. Each experience gives you the courage and understanding which you will be able to depend on when you reach out for the greater truths that are before you.

Just as children have found it necessary to accept responsibility for their studies, you also need to accept the responsibility for learning lessons that come to you while in Earth form. It is much more than simply reading the words or sitting in a classroom and listening. Words can leave as fast as they reach the ears. You alone must make the effort to retain the lesson.

Responsibility brings to us the things that are for us. You always grow stronger with each experience, and these experiences bring you closer to who you are, a child of God, a spirit being in human form.

When we complain, we attract the lower vibrations. If we think of illness, we attract illness, because if we visualize ourselves with imperfections we are sending that vibration to our consciousness. If you throw out vibrations of worry, illness, and disharmony, those thoughts will be picked up and multiplied in the ethers and will be picked up by others as well and brought back to you. That is the law of attraction. When you accept responsibility and try to work out your solution with an open heart and a positive outlook, you attract positive solutions. You open the door wide between you, your teachers, and loved ones and your higher self, allowing abundance to flow in.

Remember, the Universe is in a constant state of vibration. These vibrations are at different frequencies: some are low and some are quite high. You can think of them as musical notes. Sometimes the music is pleasing to the ears and then we have other music that hurts our ears. It is you who are in control; if you send out vibrations of worry or complaining, that is what you will attract.

Being mindful of the law of vibration, you should say, no matter what the lesson is: I will meet it with the best of my ability. By doing this, you will surround yourself with the vibration of harmony and you will also attract to yourself helpers in the physical world and the spirit world.

Remember there is no one else in the entire Universe that is responsible for you. There is no one else on the Earth or in spirit that can shoulder your responsibilities, just as you are not expected to accept the responsibility of others'. Your thoughts are always with you, as part of your life experience. Your thoughts are a product of your soul, your understanding is the midway point between you and the things you experience.

Questions to Ask Yourself

1. Have there been times when I have felt responsible for anyone else?

2. How much do I really understand the Law of Attraction?

3. Should I permit myself, through accepting responsibility, to be used by undesirable forces? Can I think of instances when this energy tried to attach to me?

4. Why is it important to channel my thoughts into constructive patterns? Can I identify an internal negative perspective that I could change into a constructive, positive one?

5. Can I think of times when I attracted similar low-vibrational energy when I was unhappy or complained? Can I remember times when my cheerful, higher vibrational energy attracted similarly positive energy?

List some of the similarities between me studying and a child going to school, and some of the differences as I see them.

Exercises for the Week

As you go through the week and interact with people, see if you can feel which chakra they are coming from and then respond to them on that energy level. This gives you a chance to go within yourself and to know yourself. It really does not have anything to do with how they are feeling, but gives you a chance to find out more about yourself. This exercise will help you to open up more to the higher consciousness within.

Notes

____

____

____

____

____

There is a need for you to exercise the thought form of your mind, just as there is a need for you to exercise the muscles of the body. You are responsible for every thought, and as you accept this, you are actually sharpening your ability to create your own reality. Believe it or not there are those in spirit who are waiting for the opportunity to return to the Earth life so they can take up the burden of personal responsibility once more.

Eternity cannot be measured because it is never ending. Even with all the years of numerous incarnations, your Earth experiences would be small in comparison to eternity. Can you realize the responsibility to yourself in this Earth life? Those on the spirit side treasure every little Earth experience that they had the opportunity to have. You will find that after you are back home in spirit, the experiences and lessons that you have had while you were on the Earth were not a tragedy at all. You take with you only your thoughts, your consciousness, and your higher self back home to spirit. It is then that you will see that only as you accepted your responsibility were you really learning. Wouldn't it be nice to know this and accept this while you are still on the Earth plane? Take the responsibility of thought and action as a part of your daily life. Be happy with working out the solutions of your daily problems and you will see the door to spirit and to your higher self open wide right before your eyes.

PHYSICAL MEDIUMSHIP

Physical **mediumship** can be a long and tedious process. You could be sitting in the circle for months or even years before anything happens. Working with ectoplasm, one needs to be extremely dedicated to their personal development as a physical medium. Every time a physical medium sets for a séance they are in danger of their own lives. This is why, in a little bit, I will spell out the do's and don'ts for various aspects of physical mediumship.

One of the reasons why there are not many physical mediums is because it takes dedication and discipline to sit in a circle for long periods of time and maybe have nothing happen. But when you do start to see results, it is all worth it. In the early days of spiritualism, people would sit in circles of 2 to 10 people, not only for development but also as a time to socialize. Most of the great pioneer mediums began by sitting in a home circle. In today's age, this is rare for people to have home circles for the development of physical mediumship. This is where dedication and discipline come in; people need to commit to show up each week at the same day and time for an hour or two, come rain or shine. In other words, there is no excuse for missing class. Class is the priority.

The word ectoplasm comes from the Greek word ektos (outside of), and plasma (something formed). The term was coined by the French physiologist Charles Richet, who at one point, had served as the president of the U.K.'s society for psychic research. The spirit operator from beyond receives a supply of etheric energy matter (ectoplasm), from the medium. Spirit people then use the ectoplasm to create an image or molding of themselves. To see the materialization of spirit is the most amazing phenomena to witness. And after spirit has walked away from the medium, you can see the cord that has formed, an umbilical cord, between the spirit and the medium. When the spirit dematerializes, the ectoplasm goes back into the body of the medium. Provided the proper conditions, there is no limit to what spirit can do. We will discuss this later on.

Years ago, in order to believe in the world beyond, people needed to see the full manifestation of spirit - as evidence. After all, seeing is believing. Even in today's age, people still want to see evidence so they can know the spiritual realm is real. As people came to accept the reality of mediumship, they yearned for the teachings of spirit and the corresponding philosophy.

Around the 1930s, physical mediumship was extremely common. The strength and range of phenomena was truly amazing. Today is quite another story. You will find a lot of working physical mediums in Europe, and there are still physical mediums in the United States, but very few. Physical mediumship takes a toll on the body and major organs due to the ectoplasm that is removed from the body of the medium. Numerous physical mediums passed away at a young age, anywhere from 24 to 34 years old, years ago. Unfortunately, they didn't have the understanding that we do today, of how physically demanding it is.

People asked: Why would anyone want to do that work? The answer is simple, for the love of spirit, the love of the work, and to show the world proof of life after death. They would do circles, sometimes 5 times a week; it would wear down the physical body. They would also not take care of their physical body, eating and drinking whatever they wanted to. Back in the 1930s, few people were health-conscious. To practice in the present, we know better. We know that the body is a Temple and we do our best to take care of ourselves in order to be the strongest possible channel for spirit to come through. And now, one practices only once or twice a week.

YOUR JOURNEY WITHIN: A Meditation To The Akashic Records

(To reflect on the week and see your spiritual growth.)

You will be taking a journey "deep within one's self" through your chakras into your very essence.

As we begin our journey, sit quietly and visualize the white light that surrounds you. Breathe it in. As you exhale, all the tension of the week and of the day melts away with each breath. Visualize the white light filling your whole body, your very essence and become aware of the warmth filling you up inside. You sink into feelings of deep relaxation and peace within yourself.

Focus on the space in between and above your eyes, on your forehead – your mind's eye – and imagine yourself entering this sacred portal. Travel back, back, back until you see a golden door. Reach out with your hand and the door will open onto a beautiful field. You are standing at the beginning of a glowing path. See the lush green grass, trees, and plants of many shapes and sizes. Hear the birds singing in the trees and gaze at the many beautiful, delicate butterflies flitting from flower to flower. The colors are vibrant. You can feel the healing energies that surround you.

Step forward on this path thru this field alive with nature's beauty and you'll see an opening in the side of a nearby hill. White light is radiating out from the opening. It draws you closer and closer. As you walk up to the white light, you know that you are about to take a journey within.

As you step through the cave opening, you notice that the walls all around you are illuminated with a healing white light. Looking further down into Mother Earth, you see a rainbow of colors blending with each other.

When you start your journey downward, you are feeling at peace.

The walls of the cave blend into a beautiful purple color. Stop for a moment. Feel the energies. You are seeing more clearly than you ever have before.

As you continue to walk downwards, the purple fuses with blue until the walls are a solid, vibrant blue. Pause here. Soak up the healing energies of the blue. Your throat feels relaxed; you know that words would flow easily and peacefully.

You travel further down into the cave, and the blue melts into green until the walls change entirely and glow with a lush green. Feeling safe, your heart opens up as it never has before. You feel the love and peace that resides within. You are fully aware of your connection to the Universe and to yourself as you stand here. Soak up the healing energy of "one's higher self."

As you continue on your journey, the green merges with yellow until you are standing in a room that is a gleaming yellow. This yellow energy surrounds you. Allow yourself to feel its loving warmth. You feel deeply at peace with yourself as you stand here soaking up this peaceful feeling.

You move forward, and the yellow begins to blend with orange, until you are standing in a room ablaze with orange. An inner knowing rises within. You understand that you can receive anything that you want, for everything is yours for the asking. Everything is possible in your life right now. Nothing is impossible. Your total being is immersed in orange energy.

Walking on, into the depths of the cave, the orange melds with red and you enter a magnificent red cavern. Feel the energy that surrounds you. You feel grounded, centered, and at one with yourself. You have reached the very essence of your being. You see stairs leading up to a golden altar. On the altar are two candles giving off a soft red glow. A book sits in the middle of the altar.

You walk up the stairs and open the book. You know, without a doubt, that this is the book of your soul's journey. This is your book, that you wrote while you were in spirit. Your Akashic Record, the blueprint of your life while on this Earth. It holds within it the pages of your past, the present, and the future. For you laid out everything to come to pass in your life before you came to the Earth plane. Now you have a chance to read what you have written for yourself. Taking a slow, deep breath, open your heart and mind, preparing yourself to receive and reconnect with this spiritual knowledge. Open the book and read what you need to know. This is why you are here.

Once you have finished gathering your information, close this living book. Walk down the stairs. Red energy fills the very essence of who you are as you start your journey upwards. Again, you see the colors blending together. The red merges into the orange until you are standing in the cave where the walls are a lustrous orange. Looking down at your feet, you see a page from the book. You pick it up and continue upwards.

As you walk along, the orange walls melt into the brilliant yellow. Glancing down by your feet, you notice another page from your living book. Bend down and pick it up.

Continuing to travel upwards, you watch the walls change from yellow to a vibrant green. You look down again and see another page from your book and pick it up.

Moving upwards, the green blends with blue, and you find yourself immersed in a blue room. You find another page from your book on the floor and pick it up.

As you continue along the path upwards, the blue walls start to shift from blue to purple. You are next surrounded by the color purple. In front of you is another page from the book, and you pick this one up too.

You see a luminescent white light radiating from the opening where you came in. There lays the last page for you to pick up. You now possess all the pages you came for on your journey.

You read the pages, standing within in the glowing white light. You know the information that you have brought back with you is from your living book. This information will serve you on your journey.

As you walk out onto the open green fields, you take to the path and drink in all the trees, the plants, the birds singing, and the butterflies that surround you. You feel at peace. You know the knowledge that you brought back with you will be remembered. As you continue to walk, you see the golden door that you entered through.

Walk back through it into your mind's eye. Go back, back into your chair, remembering all the pages you have brought back with you in your consciousness into the here and now.

You feel revitalized, alert, and wide awake, feeling as if you just had eight hours of peaceful sleep.

MESSAGE FROM SPIRIT

As we move forward in our development, spirit wants us to know that we can be as happy on Earth as in spirit, for we really do receive what we ask for. We have only to look for and make ourselves ready for greater happiness on Earth. This will come about only when we have placed ourselves in the rightful place, in the scheme of things. When one truly comes to know that our world and the spirit world are one.

Let's look at a drop of water. Where does one drop begin and the next one end, or where is one breath of air separated from another? They all merge together into the whole ocean of life. Just as there is no separation between these elements, there is no separation in the Universe. The visible and the invisible live side by side. Your world belongs to God, to yourself, to the higher consciousness which is the Universe. As certain as there is beauty in the world beyond mortal vision, there is beauty in your visible world, your life is only a reflection of your life in spirit.

The Earth we live on is like one big school ground. We have classes and recess, and sometimes we get sent to the principal's office. Let's look at two different trains of thought here. We have two people that enter the Earth plane at the same time. One sits in their seat and waits for the recess bell to ring and the other becomes very interested in their work and the progression of learning. With each new day at school, the first one is headed to drop out the minute they are permitted to do so. The second, however, will go on to college and a good career. One is simply passing through life and waiting for that recess bell to ring while the other is eager and able to learn according to his or her efforts.

Many on the Earth plane are just passing through and will need to return in order to have the same experiences for their soul's growth. We have all heard the old saying: beauty is in the eye of the beholder. An artist who has trained their eyes to look for the beauty in everything will find it, even if it is a pile of rubbish or a homeless person sitting on the bench, as easily as if it were a beautiful landscape. You are the artist in your life. Paint yourself a beautiful picture. Look for the beauty within, go to that higher consciousness - the higher self, and thank God, the Universe, the Earth plane for the privilege of beholding this beauty that surrounds you and that is within you.

On your journey through this Earth plane, you will find that you serve your soul's growth in many different ways; all of life is meaningful. You set up lessons for your soul's growth. This is how you progress to the higher consciousness of the higher self. The soul itself desires certain experiences that can only be gained on this Earth plane.

If you wish to progress, you first must go within to connect with that higher self. Progression can only come from the amount of effort you put forth. Do not sit back and wait for it, or expect it to be handed to you. You are a great soul, literally, with the Universe at your fingertips.

THE ELEMENTS OF THE BODY

There are 16 known elements contained in the physical body. The way these elements combine, and the degrees to which they are combined are two of the reasons all mediums do not attain the same degree or phase of Mediumship.

1. Oxygen
2. Hydrogen
3. Nitrogen
4. Carbon
5. Calcium
6. Phosphorous
7. Chlorine
8. Magnesium
9. Sulphur
10. Fluorine
11. Sodium
12. Potassium
13. Iron
14. Silicon
15. Iodine
16. Manganese

The Formula of Ectoplasm

The formula of ectoplasm was analyzed by Dr. Schrenck Von Notzing. He found it to contain:

1. Sodium
2. Chlorine
3. Oxygen
4. Phosphorus
5. Calcium
6. Nitrogen
7. Hydrogen
8. Carbon

Your Chemist Doctor

(Within your Personal Inner Band of Guides and Teachers)

Your chemist doctor takes care of the chemical process of preparing the substance in the body. They are responsible for the blending of the chemicals and the blending of the auras. This is necessary for the medium to function properly.

HOW TO SET UP A CIRCLE

1. Prepare yourself about an hour before the circle begins by going into meditation to call in your protectors, Angels and teachers. You may want to get some sage and do a blessing, but keep in mind that some people may be allergic to sage so you can also use incense or sprinkle salt around the room. The salt will absorb any negative energies. Remind the people in your group that there is no alcohol before the circle as this lowers the vibration. It only takes one person with a negative thought to stop the phenomena from happening or causing harm to the sitter. Everyone that agrees to be in the circle needs to make a commitment to one another and to spirit to show up for the circle consistently - at the same day and time scheduled. Remember, for physical phenomena you need to have dedication and discipline and a group of 4 to 12 people.
2. It is recommended to house some of the elements: water, fire (which can be a candle), air (you can have a feather for that one), and a flower for grounding.
3. You need to have the room blacked out.
4. Place everyone in a circle. The person in charge of the circle needs to tune into the energy of the participants. Sometimes people need to move around for proper balance of the energy.

5. Remind everyone to turn their cell phones off. You don't want any disturbance that may   shock the medium and cause that person harm.
6. Start with an opening prayer, or you may choose to have everyone do a silent prayer.
7. Do a 15-to-20-minute guided meditation.

At the end of the Circle, always do a closing prayer.

WAYS THE SPIRIT USES ECTOPLASM

How to tell when the ectoplasm is building up in the room during a physical Circle and some of the ways that spirit uses the ectoplasm.

You will feel the room getting a little cooler. It usually starts around the feet and the ankles and rises up. You'll feel the coolness, especially when spirit steps close to you. You may also feel a thickness of energy building up in the room and round you.

There may be different smells, possibly like an old musty sock or the smell of tobacco. It's usually a scent that's associated with that spirit or spirits that come into the Circle.

Ectoplasm varies in strength and intensity. Here are just a few of the ways that spirits use ectoplasm during a physical mediumship Circle:

1. **Raps and taps**. These can be heard all around the room, coming from any surface. When this happens, you can ask yes and no questions and spirit will answer. Usually, one rap for a yes and 2 for no. Or you may hear loud cracks: on the tables, in a chair, or even in the ceiling.

2. **Moving of bells**. If you have bells hanging from the ceiling, spirit will come and move the bells so that they are heard.

3. **Levitation**. Ectoplasm may even be used for the levitation of small objects or large objects, such as chairs and people.

4. **Direct spirit writing**, also known as slate writing. This is where a piece of paper or tablet is left in the room during the Circle. When the Circle is over, there is writing on the paper or tablet.

5. **Automatic writing**. And there is a difference between automatic writing and inspirational writing. With automatic writing, spirit places the energy or ectoplasm over the hand of the writer. You could be watching TV or reading a book and spirit could come in and write a message. With inspirational writing. you are aware, and spirit brings in thought patterns which you write down.

6. **Apports**. These are objects that are brought into the séance room from elsewhere during a sitting. Spirit can de-materialize the object from one area and then re-materialize the object into another room.

7. **Spirit lights**. These may be different sizes of lights flashing a variety of colors. Sometimes you will see orbs, balls of energy, of different shapes, sizes, and colors.

8. **Transfiguration**. This is when a mask of ectoplasm covers the medium's face.

9. **Direct voice.** This is called a trumpet Circle, which utilizes a. cone-like megaphone, usually made of aluminum. In pioneer days, some were made of different types of wood. They would levitate up in mid-air and you would hear a loved one or a teacher coming through the trumpet with messages.

10. **Independent voice**. Spirit will build a voice box and you will hear the voices coming from the corners of the room, and it will be as clear as talking to the person next to you.

TABLE TIPPING

The practice of physical mediumship is a way to help us understand the truth that the Earth plane is only one phase of life and there is no lasting separation. For example, hearing a recognized voice from beyond and having discussed matters known only to the two persons conversing, brings a solid conviction of the continuity of life. It is a way of helping us trust that the soul is eternal.

Beginning Physical Mediumship

Table tipping is considered the beginning stage of physical mediumship. Here is where we get a better idea of the ectoplasm and how the energy works. Back in the mid or late 1800s, after a day of working in the kitchen, the workers would clean the table off and prepare it for a Circle.

As mentioned earlier, this was a way of socializing. Everyone would get together with a qualified medium and they would have table tipping circles in the evening, getting together two to three times per week. Also in the early days, mediums conversed with spirit by means of raps. This was done through the use of the alphabet: one rap for the first letter and two for the second, and so on through the whole alphabet. This was one method of forming a code for conversation with spirit.

Raps and table tipping are considered the beginning of physical phenomena that help ectoplasm come from all orifices of the body. The medium must have the necessary chemicals in his or her body to produce the required power for the manifestation.

Sometimes, instead of hearing raps on the table or coming from the corners of the room, the table would tip back and forth and sometimes levitate. This occurs when spirit forms an ectoplasm rod. Usually, during a circle, you can see the ectoplasm rods being formed. They are circular, different heights, and thickness. The medium and spirit forces must learn to work together to guarantee significant power to call attention to the fact that there is an intelligent force beyond the Earth plane.

How to Pick Out Your Table

Over the years, spirit has led me to many different places to discover the perfect table. I would always look for one that had three legs. When you are first starting out, it is a little easier to get the table rocking back and forth with three legs versus four. As you advance, you can move up to four legs and a little heavier table. Initially, you want to practice with a little lighter table. I love to go antique shopping. I would go to antique stores to check out the different types of tables they had. Then I would pick out the table through psychometry. By putting my hand on the table and reading the energy, I would get a sense of the history of the table. Not only does it make for a fun day but it also gives you a chance to work on your spiritual abilities.

Other places I visited were Target, Walmart, or Bed, Bath and Beyond. I would look for the three-legged table; I believe they call them a wine table, and they're usually made up of particle board. The cost is low, $15 to $20. These make great beginner tables.

There are a couple of things to do once you get your table home. If you decided to go with the three-legged one made out of particle board, you also need to pick up some Gorilla Glue. The glue is for the legs when you screw them to secure the legs so that the table will last longer. Let it sit for at least 24 hours.

How to Cleanse and Prepare Your Table

First, you may want to give your table a name. This helps to develop a connection between you and the table. Next, pick out a nice spot for it. Remember, you will only be using it for table tipping. It's best to avoid placing any books or anything else on top of the table. The reason for this is that everything is energy. You want to build up the energy on the table, blending only your energies with it.

Some of the things that you will need for cleansing your table: apple cider vinegar and a clean or new cloth. First you will wipe down your table with the apple cider vinegar, in a counterclockwise direction. This helps with the removal of old energy. Ask that the old energies be cleansed from the table.

Next, you will say a prayer as you continue to wipe down the table in a clockwise direction, which helps to energize the table. The prayer can be anything from the Lord's prayer to a prayer of the heart. Ask that your energies be blended at this time.

Spend a little time getting to know your teachers that will be working with you. Learn the energy of the table. Learn to start feeling the energies around you.

When you first start working with the table, spend anywhere from fifteen to twenty minutes at a time, from two to three times a week. Some people get the table up and running their first time out. Other times it could take anywhere from seven to fourteen days. Do not get discouraged. This is the reason we suggest fifteen to twenty minutes per sitting.

There can be anywhere from one person to four people at a time on the table. You can sit at nighttime or daytime but when you first start, do your best to be consistent on the time. After all, you are making an appointment with spirit. You will want to place your hands lightly on top of the table. The energy runs through the palm chakras and attaches to the nervous system in the second chakra. As you get more proficient, you will be able to remove your hand from the table and the table will continue to tip and even levitate.

One of the reasons I love working with the table is that it shows there is something beyond the physical world. The table works as a battery. It will amplify your abilities. Say one of your abilities is clear hearing or clear seeing - by using the table you will strengthen your abilities.

You may want to write down your questions before you begin. The reason for this is when the table gets going, it seems like all questions and thought patterns go right out the window; you draw a blank. Remember this Earth plane is a school ground. Sometimes we are in the classroom studying, other times we are outside playing, and sometimes we get sent to the principal›s office. This your spiritual journey. Enjoy it. Many blessings.

Questions to Ask Yourself

Should the world be regarded as a place of trouble or should we regard it as a place of opportunity for growth?

____

____

____

____

Spirit tells us this is all one world. Do I see the world as divided into two parts, seen and unseen?

____

____

____

____

Do I think some close friends or teachers or guides can hand me my spiritual development?

____

____

____

____

Are any of us complete unto ourselves?

____

____

____

____

There's an old saying: *The laborer has to work if he wants to eat.* How am I using this saying as regards my own spiritual growth?[55]

Thoughts About Our Creator's Love

Everyone is on their own spiritual journey. We all have different spiritual lessons and growth to learn in different ways. We have different people that join us on our journey, sometimes for an hour, a day, 10 to 20 years or even a lifetime. But once those spiritual lessons (contracts) are learned, we thank those people for helping us and move forward. How do we know the spiritual contract has been fulfilled? You might not see things in the same way anymore or agree on things that you used to agree on. Your consciousness has changed and you look at things differently. You look at the way you see yourself now and their consciousness has stayed the same. Their thinking has not changed. That's okay there is no wrong or right. It's a matter of have you learned your spiritual lesson and completed your spiritual contract with that individual?

Another way to look at it is: you move into a beautiful apartment or house that meets all your needs and you sign a contract saying yes I will live here for a year. After a year, you go back and look at how happy you have or have not been. You may say to yourself, this place served the purpose for the time being but I have changed. This place (or person) no longer serves a purpose for my best and highest good. I have outgrown this place. At the time it helped with your spiritual growth but now it's time for a bigger place. A place that suits your needs better as you grow body, mind and soul. I believe that if people would look at their soul contracts in a spiritual way, their physical life would be a little easier. When we look at things with the spiritual eye, not only do we have an understanding of the why's and how's from a spiritual viewpoint, but we also have an understanding from a human perspective. It's easier when we have the understanding of the what's and how's of this beautiful journey choosing to come down to earth to live this experience.

Remember, this earth is a spiritual school and classroom. We are down here for our soul's growth. To have spiritual lessons and to fulfill our spiritual contracts. At times we are in the classroom studying, sometimes we're on the playground having fun and playing with friends and other times we get sent to the principal's office.

Just as we learn lessons in school so we can progress to the next grade, we have teachers and classmates that help us with the human mind and spiritual world. They help us progress to the next level. Sometimes they hang around for a lifetime, other times they had their own spiritual journey they needed to go and fulfill. Just as they have helped us to grow, we have helped them to. It is always 50-50, never just one way so we give thanks to them and ourselves for the spiritual and conscious growth. And we continue to keep moving forward on this beautiful spiritual journey.

This is your homework if you will, so you may graduate to the next level and continue your journey for spiritual enlightenment.

Remember to always look at everything with your spiritual eye. It does not mean that you will not have to go through spiritual growth, but it does mean you will have an understanding and knowledge for the reason behind it.

I wish you may blessings, dear ones,

Felice Izzarelli

In this book Felice Izzarelli uses mantras and chants to help you *Find the Magic in You!* It is your chance to learn to reconnect with the vibrations of your chakras, the major energy centers of your body, and open up to a new level within yourself. You will learn to see your chakras, their colors, where they are located, and how you can change your life by better understanding them.

Felice shares his knowledge by teaching others how to reach their true potential by building relationships with our guides. His teachings help others along their intuitive path of self discovery, while in turn helping them become teachers of spiritual knowledge.

The more we spread this word, Felice advocates, and the more we share what we've learned with others, the more we raise our own consciousness to the spiritual world around us. In turn, students teach their teachers important life lessons and the positive progression continues.

Felice comes from a family of teachers and spiritual guides. His grandmother, an amazing woman, channeled Sir Isaac Newton who spent the latter part of his life creating inventions that work as physical conductors between the two worlds. Even back in the 1800s he understood the deep connection between the spiritual and physical worlds.

In like fashion, Felice instructs throughout the world via his internet videos, through publishing, and by making available the original recordings of his grandmother.

Much of what he learned is found in his books like this one. "Are you ready to *Find the Magic in You?*"

Available at Amazon and your local bookseller.

Acknowledgments

First, I thank spirit for their teachings and the unconditional love they share with me. I thank them for the teachings of the spirit world, most especially for the understanding that there is no death - only the next steppingstone on one's spiritual journey.

In turn I am blessed to share their teachings with my students so I can help them along their spiritual journey.

I would like to especially thank three strong women. One was my grandmother who did the work of spiritual teaching for 80 years and who showed me how to develop a strong connection with spirit.

Thanks to my mother, a strong woman who helped me to have an open heart and who gave me the inner strength to move forward. She helped me see the beauty in all God's creation always she had a heart open to kindness.

Thirdly, thanks to Sara, a strong and loving woman who is part of my soul family and who always seeks to help another. Sara brings Christ's light to everyone she meets, be it a child, or a woman, or a man or an animal. Sara helps remind me to see the good in a person and to remember that we are all on a spiritual journey. She helped me have an open heart so I can see the light that shines bright within each of us.

When I think of Sara, I'm reminded of the old saying that there is nothing so strong as gentleness, and nothing so gentle as the real strength within each of us.

In different ways, each of these three women have shown me unconditional love. Each in their unique way helped me see that to be vulnerable is a strength that adds a great deal to my soul and life.

Finally, let me dedicate this book also to all my students. They have shown me how to be a better person and spiritual teacher. I am truly blessed to have known each and every one of you.

With all my love,
Felice

About Rev. Felice Izzarelli

There are but a few people left who are descendants from the first families of the original spiritualist movement which spread rapidly throughout America during the mid-1800s. These families once lived together in thriving societies and gathered in spiritualist churches for nearly two-hundred years. Today, as a new generation of members have discovered the communities, many original descendants of this rich heritage continue to devote themselves to seeking lives of self-growth.

Felice Izzarelli is a man born into such a family. He was raised by strong and gifted grandparents, Alvina Davis and Kenneth Davis and by his mother, Ruth Izzarelli. He learned early in life that Spirit is directing us always, and that all we have to do is listen. One of the lessons he is grateful to have learned is that true strength is taught through gentleness and love. He was taught the secrets of how prayers and vibrations work in the universe. His mother and grandmother taught young Felice that there is no death; how to reach out to his guides who brought him comfort through lessons learned and who gave him the strength and wisdom to teach others.

It took him nearly half a lifetime to learn to truly tap in and reach out to teachers in this realm. His path led him to develop his physical body and emotions through mastering martial arts, which in turn prepared Felice for the development of his relationship to the spiritual world. He found a Teacher at Harmony Grove who built upon the foundation of knowledge of physical and spiritualist mediumship that his grandmother and mother had provided decades before.

Felice shares what he learned by teaching others how to reach their potential. He helps others build relationships with the guides who direct our intuitive path of self-discovery, guides who help us develop as teachers of spiritualist knowledge. Felice knows that the more we spread the word and help others teach, the more we raise our consciousness to the spirit world around us. In turn, students teach their teachers important life lessons.

Felice was an instructor and served as the Director of Education at Harmony Grove Spiritualist Association, a 166 year-old spiritualist community. He teaches throughout the world via workshops, through publishing and by making available the original recordings of Gordon Burroughs who channeled Physicist Dr. sir Isaac Newton. Dr. Newton knew back in the 1800s that there was a deep connection between the spiritual and physical worlds and spent the latter part of his life creating inventions to work as physical conduits between these worlds.

Now 67, Felice Izzarelli also spent 30 years studying and teaching martial arts. This discipline has helped him master the ability to direct energy through self control and meditation. Felice has taught martial arts since 1987 to help others employ its disciplines as they develop their own spiritual practice.

His love for healing and teaching others led him to continue his education and in 2003 he become an ordained Spiritualist minister reverend in the field of spiritual studies mediumship and universal law. He is called to be an instrument through which healing energy flows.

Felice is devoted to teaching spiritual development and assisting in the process of healing through the release of pain and suffering. He specializes in Physical Mediumship and healing. He teaches classes and holds workshops on Physical Mediumship, Healing, Clairvoyance, Transfiguration, Out of Body Experience, Tarot cards, Clairaudio, Reiki, Psychometry, Table Tipping, Cord Cutting and Clairsentience.

Felice offers spiritual counseling, Spiritual mentoring, and does one-on-one readings and provides certifications in Reiki, Clairaudio, Clairvoyance, Clairsentience, and Healing.

For more information about Felice Izzarelli and how he can help you enrich your life by developing your physical and spiritual mediumship skills, please contact him at 760-580-9459